Contents

What is air?

Air is all around us.

You cannot see, smell, or taste air.

You can feel air on a windy day.

You can feel air on a swing.

Living things and air

People, other animals, and plants are living things.

People, other animals, and plants
need air.

Breathing

People and other animals breathe in
the air they need.

Most animals breathe through their nose and mouth.

Insects breathe through tiny holes in their bodies.

gill

Fish breathe through holes
called gills.

Plants do not breathe like people.

Plants take in air through tiny holes in their leaves.

Why do living things need air?

People and other animals need air to stay alive.

Plants need air to stay alive, too.

People need air to keep their bodies working.

Other animals need air to keep their
bodies working, too.

Plants need air, sunlight, and water to make food.

Plants need air to grow.

Air quiz

Which of these things does not need air?

Answer on page 24

Picture glossary

 **breathe** take air into and out of the body

 **gill** part of a fish that helps it breathe

 **insect** animal with six legs, such as a beetle

 **living thing** something that is alive, such as an animal or a plant

Index

Answer to question on page 22
The frog and the flowers need air.
The toy train does not need air.

Notes for parents and teachers
Before reading
Collect pictures showing examples of living and non-living things, for example, animals including humans, plants, bricks, pencils, books. Explain to the children that all living things breathe air and grow. Show them the pictures and ask them to determine which things they think are living and which are non-living. Can the children think of other examples?

After reading
• Take the children outside and ask them if they can feel the air on their faces. Do they know which way the wind is blowing? Ask the children to each dip a finger into a jug of water and hold it up in the air. They should turn round slowly, and when they feel their finger is colder they should stop. Explain that they are now facing the way the wind is blowing. The air is making their finger cooler.

• Fill a container with a solution of one part water with two parts washing up liquid. Make loops out of thin wire. Invite the children to dip the loops into the liquid and then blow gently. What happens? What did they do to make the bubbles?